Little People, BIG DREAMS
JANE GOODALL

Written by
Mª Isabel Sánchez Vegara

Illustrated by
Beatrice Cerocchi

Lincoln
Children's Books

When Jane was a little girl, her father gave her a stuffed chimpanzee named Jubilee. She carried him wherever she went.

Jane loved animals very much. She wanted to live
in the jungle with wild chimpanzees, just like the
heroes of her bedtime stories: Tarzan and Jane.
At night, her mother read her their adventures.

But Jane could not afford to go to college to study
animals. So, she would have to study them in her
own way. She saved every penny she had until
she could buy a boat ticket to Kenya, in Africa.

When she arrived, Jane met a well-known scientist named Louis Leakey. He was looking for a chimpanzee researcher willing to study them in the wild. He thought that they could learn about humans by studying apes. It was the opportunity Jane had been waiting for!

So, Jane took another journey to the shores of Gombe, in Tanzania. To start with, she couldn't see any chimpanzees, but she had the feeling that they were near, watching her...

She decided to sit quietly in the same spot, day after day. Finally, a small group of chimpanzees appeared, and let her sit with them. Jane had been accepted into the family!

Instead of numbering them, as all the other scientists did, Jane decided to give every chimpanzee a name. There was David Greybeard, Flo, Flint, Fifi, and Gigi, to name a few!

By watching them carefully, she noticed that some chimps were kind, quiet, and generous, while others were bullies. It seemed that humans and chimps were not so different, after all.

Then Jane made another incredible discovery: chimpanzees could make their own tools! This was something only humans were thought to do.

Jane's talent was quickly recognized by Cambridge University.
Here, she studied for her doctorate in animal behavior.
And it wasn't long before she wrote her first article
for one of the most famous science magazines.

Jane continued to study chimps in the Gombe for forty years. But jungles were starting to disappear across Africa, which put all animals in danger. She knew she had to do something!

Jane joined countless projects to protect nature. She was no longer just a courageous researcher, but also the most determined wildlife defender the world had ever seen.

And the little girl who loved animals challenges us to be kind to nature. Because if chimpanzees can live in harmony with their environment, we can, too.

JANE GOODALL

(Born 1934 – Present)

c. 1935

c. 1940

Jane Goodall was born in London, England. When she was one, her father gave her a cuddly toy chimpanzee, named Jubilee. Some people thought it would scare her, but she loved it, and it fostered her early love of animals. From an early age, Jane dreamed of living in Africa, where she could watch and write about animals. Jane's mother encouraged her dream and told her she must never give up. But when Jane left school, she couldn't afford to go to college to follow her dream. So, she worked hard to save enough money, and in 1957, she traveled to Kenya, in Africa. There, she met with a very important scientist named Dr. Louis Leakey, who was so impressed with Jane that he hired her as his assistant. Jane

1965   1995

traveled to the Gombe Stream chimpanzee reserve in Tanzania to
study chimps in the wild. At first, it was hard to get close enough to
study them. But Jane waited patiently every day, giving them their
space. Soon, they accepted her. By watching them closely, Jane
made many groundbreaking discoveries: most importantly, she saw
chimps making and using tools. This was something only humans
were thought to do. Jane showed that there isn't a sharp divide
between humans and primates, after all. Later, Jane studied for her
doctorate and became a world-leading expert on chimpanzees. Now
Jane dedicates her life to conservation and education, spreading the
message that we can all make a difference to the future of our planet.

Want to find out more about **Jane Goodall?**
Read one of these great books:

I Am Jane Goodall by Brad Meltzer and Christopher Eliopoulos
Who Is Jane Goodall? by Roberta Edwards and John O'Brien
The Watcher by Jeanette Winter

Learn how you can help Jane Goodall make the world a better place through her worldwide
program for young people of all ages: Roots & Shoots. The Roots & Shoots program has groups in
more than 100 countries—kids from kindergarten to college—all working on projects of their own
choosing to improve their communities.

Brimming with creative inspiration, how-to projects, and useful
information to enrich your everyday life, Quarto Knows is a favorite
destination for those pursuing their interests and passions. Visit our
site and dig deeper with our books into your area of interest:
Quarto Creates, Quarto Cooks, Quarto Homes, Quarto Lives,
Quarto Drives, Quarto Explores, Quarto Gifts, or Quarto Kids.

Text © 2018 Mª Isabel Sánchez Vegara. Illustrations © 2018 Beatrice Cerocchi.
First Published in the UK in 2018 by Lincoln Children's Books, an imprint of The Quarto Group.
400 First Avenue North, Suite 400, Minneapolis, MN 55401, USA.
T (612) 344-8100 F (612) 344-8692 **www.QuartoKnows.com**
First Published in Spain in 2018 under the title Pequeña & Grande Jane Goodall
by Alba Editorial, s.l.u., Baixada de Sant Miquel, 1, 08002 Barcelona
www.albaeditorial.es
All rights reserved.
Published by arrangement with Alba Editorial, s.l.u. Translation rights arranged by IMC Agència Literària, SL
All rights reserved.
No part of this publication may be reproduced, stored in a retrieval system, or transmitted, in any form, or by any
means, electrical, mechanical, photocopying, recording or otherwise without the prior written permission of the
publisher or a license permitting restricted copying.

ISBN 978-1-78603-231-7
The illustrations were created with gouache and pastels. Set in Futura BT.

Published by Rachel Williams • Designed by Karissa Santos
Edited by Katy Flint • Production by Jenny Cundill

Manufactured in Guangdong, China CC092018

9 7 5 3 1 2 4 6 8

Photographic acknowledgements (pages 28–29, from left to right) 1. Jane Goodall with Jubilee, c. 1935 © the Jane Goodall Institute / Courtesy
of the Goodall Family 2. Jane Goodall with cat, c. 1940 © the Jane Goodall Institute / Courtesy of the Goodall Family 3. Jane Goodall in
Gombe Stream National Park, Tanzania, 1965 © CBS Photo Archive via Getty Images 4. Jane Goodall, English primatologist, ethologist, and
anthropologist with a chimpanzee in her arms, 1995 © Apic via Getty Images

MIX
Paper from
responsible sources
FSC® C008047

Collect the *Little People,* BIG DREAMS series:

FRIDA KAHLO

ISBN: 978-1-84780-783-0

COCO CHANEL

ISBN: 978-1-84780-784-7

MAYA ANGELOU

ISBN: 978-1-84780-889-9

AMELIA EARHART

ISBN: 978-1-84780-888-2

AGATHA CHRISTIE
ISBN: 978-1-84780-960-5

MARIE CURIE

ISBN: 978-1-84780-962-9

ROSA PARKS

ISBN: 978-1-78603-018-4

AUDREY HEPBURN

ISBN: 978-1-78603-053-5

EMMELINE PANKHURST

ISBN: 978-1-78603-020-7

ELLA FITZGERALD

ISBN: 978-1-78603-087-0

ADA LOVELACE

ISBN: 978-1-78603-076-4

JANE AUSTEN

ISBN: 978-1-78603-120-4

GEORGIA O'KEEFFE

ISBN: 978-1-78603-122-8

HARRIET TUBMAN

ISBN: 978-1-78603-227-0

ANNE FRANK

ISBN: 978-1-78603-229-4

MOTHER TERESA

ISBN: 978-1-78603-230-0

JOSEPHINE BAKER

ISBN: 978-1-78603-228-7

L. M. MONTGOMERY

ISBN: 978-1-78603-233-1

JANE GOODALL

ISBN: 978-1-78603-231-7

SIMONE DE BEAUVOIR

ISBN: 978-1-78603-232-4

Now in board book format:

COCO CHANEL

ISBN: 978-1-78603-245-4

MAYA ANGELOU

ISBN: 978-1-78603-249-2

FRIDA KAHLO

ISBN: 978-1-78603-247-8

AMELIA EARHART

ISBN: 978-1-78603-251-5

MARIE CURIE

ISBN: 978-1-78603-253-9